MANIPULATED

BY

H G TUDOR

COPYRIGHT 2015
All Rights Reserved

Manipulated

By

H G Tudor

All rights reserved. No part of this book may be reproduced, or stored in a retrieval system, or transmitted in any form or by any means, electronic, mechanical, photocopying, recording, or otherwise, without the express written permission of the publisher.

Published by Insight Books

First Edition 2015

Dedications

To those who read and in so doing become better armed

Introduction

Hello. I have returned and this time I am going to tell you about twenty-five ways in which I manipulate you. Yes, the inside track on twenty-five nefarious methods by which I exert my control over you. It is fascinating material and absolutely imperative reading for anybody who wants a relationship, is in a relationship or is recovering from an abusive relationship. That pretty much includes most people on the planet. That's the level of danger we are dealing with here. This material is not just applicable to my kind and me, the narcissists, but those who engage in abusive behaviour. Thus it includes those who suffer from borderline personality disorder as they engage in manipulative behaviour as well, those who suffer from anti-social personality disorder, the alcoholics and the drug abusers and people who may not suffer a disorder or an addiction but nevertheless have traits which cause them to engage in manipulative behaviour. Just because somebody engages in a few of these behaviour does not mean they have a personality disorder or they are an addict who is trying to manipulate you so they receive their fix and get you to do what they want. What is does mean though is that if you recognise these behaviours you are dealing with a manipulative individual. If you recognise many of these forms of manipulation then it is highly likely you are dealing with a disordered individual and probably one of my kind, the narcissist. The purpose of this book is to allow you to recognise which behaviour is manipulative, confirm your own suspicions and allow you to understand why it is being used against you so you can then defend yourself.

You will learn twenty-five methods by which I get you to do what I want. It is going to thrill, chill and make you feel ill. Fortunately for you, by reading this, you will be equipped to avoid lasting damage.

I am a narcissist. I am completely aware of this. Those people who suggest that my kind and me do not know what we are doing have been fooled. We are entirely aware of what we do and what our words and behaviours cause. Unfortunately for those outside of our select circle, we do not care about the consequences of our actions. Why is this? Briefly, it is because we are driven by an all-consuming need for fuel. This need is so absolute, so rampant and never-ending that any consideration of the results of our actions falls a distant second to the need to obtain fuel. We are entitled to this fuel and this means that we leave behind a legacy of chaos and confusion. We do not have the time to consider what we have done. We must secure the next source of our fuel. If this collateral damage is a necessary effect of obtaining our fuel then it must be so.

    What is this fuel? It is attention and emotional reaction. Your focus and admiration must be on me at all times. I crave that attention. I want that attention. I need that attention. I need the emotional reaction from you and from other people. Without it I am nothing. I cease to exist. The form of your reaction does not matter, so long as it is directed at me. Some reactions provide more fuel than others and it also improves dependent on who is supplying this fuel. Initially it will be in the form of love, affection and admiration as you succumb to my world-renown powers of seduction. I make you feel ultra-happy so that you pour your positive emotions all over me and it feels magnificent. All of that creates sweet, and potent fuel. After a time, your attention and reactions will be transmuted into anger, tears, hatred, confusion and bewilderment. All of those states of mind and more work for me. As long as I cause your tears, so long as I can see you sobbing because of what I have done. So long as you are shouting at me in order to berate me for my flagrant abusive behaviour. As long as you are begging me to recognise what I have done. It is all attention and emotional reaction and that equates to fuel.

How do I secure these reactions and consequently my fuel? The answer can be found in one word; manipulation. I am the world champion of manipulation. I am the puppet master. Machiavelli has nothing on my machinations. Why am I so absolutely brilliant at manipulation? It is because I do it all the time; every moment of every day I am manipulating those around me. I have honed this skill over years of practice. Each day I have extended my tendrils and slid them around people as I bring them around to my way of thinking. I have them doing what I want, when I want and doing so repeatedly.

I weave my magic and they become spellbound. They are caught in my created reality where you cannot escape and thus become a chess piece in the game that I and only I control. I am the consummate professional of applying manipulative techniques. Manipulation is my key skill and like any dedicated craftsman you must exercise it, practise it and wield it in order to hone it and make it more effective. Thousands of people have fallen prey to my manipulative techniques. Lovers, family members, friends, colleagues, acquaintances, service providers, helpers, volunteers, lawyers, judges, law enforcers and even strangers.

The fascinating thing about my manipulative skills is that those who are subject to them do not even realise that they have been manipulated until it is far too late. By then I have extracted what I have wanted and moved on, leaving you swinging in the breeze and a shadow of your former self. The covert behaviours I utilise are extremely effective. When they are exercised, they appear often as something else and thus you are unaware that they are being deployed. That is until now.

This book details twenty-five manipulative techniques that I regularly use. I explain how I do it and the effect it generates which will ultimately lead to me getting what I want; my fuel. You will notice that many of these techniques can become interwoven to provide maximum effectiveness. In some instances, the use of one manipulative technique then paves the way from the other. They are all interconnected in some way, which often makes it harder for you to distinguish what I am doing and how I am doing it. It all seems part of your way of life. It is the false world that I create for you to exist in and the one where I am king and the Supreme Authority.

Thus, you will be privy to these malevolent and insidious wiles. Being the decent and honest person you are, you ought to notify everyone you know of to familiarise themselves with my techniques so that they are forewarned. You should be providing copies of this book to everybody you care about and love. If you have been manipulated already, you will recognise much of what I write and perhaps it will aid your understanding as to why it happened. It may even remove the shame you feel at realising what has happened to you. It will certainly ensure that it will not happen again and therefore amounts to an invaluable resource to protect yourself and those you care for.

Why would I tell the world the secret of my technique? Surely that would defeat me and thus deny me the very thing that I need? That actually is not the case. Foolishly, not everyone will read this and furthermore, there are always those who read but do not retain. There will be plenty of people utterly unaware whose strings I will still jerk and pull. They will always dance for me.

In common with my usual style, I do not pull any punches. I do not go in for convoluted scientific explanations. There are other publications, which do that and do it well, but it is not required here. This is about you getting to understand the manipulative techniques that my kind and me regularly deploy to devastating effect and enabling you to learn them quickly and easily. You are benefiting from this knowledge being drawn straight from the source. It is not filtered or diluted but provided to you in an accessible form and one, which provides a very useful point of reference. By all means, go down the rabbit hole and explore these techniques further. You can ascertain more about why my kind and me do these things and you can also learn more about recovering from the effect of being subjected to these techniques. There are plenty of people out there who will help you heal. I am not a healer. I am the problem but with that there comes knowledge and understanding far more effective than any bystander. I know what I am. I know what I do and I am best placed to tell you exactly how I will manipulate you once you come within my sphere of influence.

1. Love Bombing

I am going to begin with love bombing for several reasons. First of all, it is used at the outset of my manipulation of you. Secondly, it is a massively successful manipulative tool and thirdly it paves the way for the deployment and use of several other manipulative techniques. Fourthly, if you are clued in to this tried and tested narcissistic technique then you may just get away from me (admittedly it is very difficult but it could happen) and thus you will avoid being subjected to all of the other methods below. Moreover, you will save your sanity, your self-esteem, your money and your health. Accordingly, being switched on to love bombing is essential. In fact, if everyone who is about to start their dating journey was made aware of love-bombing there would be far, far fewer narcissistic casualties. It deservedly belongs at the top of the twenty-five. I often think that the technique of love bombing ought to be taught in some sort of relationships and social skills class at schools. At that age people have little experience of relationships and therefore would not be able to distinguish whether certain behaviour is normal or not. It becomes all the more difficult when that behaviour is pleasant, wonderful and addictive. Highlighting awareness of what love bombing is and what it does would be a useful role for the educators in society.

The primary purpose of love bombing is to win your confidence. It overrides your cautionary instincts and critical thinking so I can control you. It also serves a number of secondary purposes, which I utilise in other forms of manipulation, which I describe in greater detail below. Love bombing enables me to also: -

- Condition you to expect affection so I can later withdraw it;
- Lower your defences and thus make you more susceptible to my manipulation;
- Generate a golden period, which I will utilise at the later stages;
- Ensure you open up to me about your life so I gain knowledge about every facet of your life for later exploitation (e.g. what you like so I can apply this to continue the seduction and then your weaknesses so I know how to hurt you)

- Send a signal to a discarded victim that I have someone new and I am happy and thus hurt the existing victim even further

Thus, not only do I draw you in and gain your complete confidence, I am also able to prepare the groundwork for further but different forms of manipulation. It really is a magnificent form of manipulation.

The phrase love bombing arose from the Unification Church of the United States in the 1970s, better known as the Moonies. It then became a modus operandi of various cults, which used it to ensnare new recruits who showed an interest in the cult. Then, it was a highly co-ordinated approach designed to ensure that established members of the cult flooded recruits with flattery, affection and attention. Now it has become a phrase associated with the initial stage of when I make my play for you.

Love bombing is a repeated (it would be constant if we didn't have to sleep) bombardment of communication towards you that is brimming with beautiful words and actions. It is an avalanche of desire, a blitzkrieg of affection and a tsunami of love. It feels completely overwhelming and so it should. We want to sweep you off your feet. This communication comes in many forms and the advancement of technology has turned into a narcissist's toolkit when it comes to unleashing the barrage of love bombs.

I will repeatedly text you; in fact the level of text messages that I will send to you is excessive. You should expect to receive several hundred texts a day. We will telephone you, leave lovely voicemail messages (even though we know you wouldn't be available as we want you to come back to your 'phone to hear something delightful) and we will send copious amounts of emails. Your social media will become a bulletin board for our desire with your posts and photos always liked and always commented on in a positive manner. It will not take long before every text that arrives from us will have your heart skip a beat in anticipation of the loving message that has been contained. I will aim to spend every moment I can with you, taking you out for lunch, appearing at your work-place without warning for a drink after work, calling by at your house, arranging repeated dates and ensuring that I am by your side as often as I can. I say the most delightful things to you and take you to special places so that you want to spend all this time with me. Who wouldn't want to be subjected to this repeated praise and flattery?

We also have a penchant for sniffing out people who will be the most susceptible to our overtures. I am brilliant at reading body language and knowing how people think. As I mentioned in the introduction, this is because I do this often and repeatedly in order to polish my manipulative skills. Accordingly, I say and do exactly what you want so it has an enhanced effect. I look for people who have been in abusive relationships previously in order to ensnare them. If you have been hurt previously then this tells me two things.

The first is that you have most likely been damaged by one of my kind already and therefore that means my techniques will work. Yes, I am afraid that lightning does strike twice. Secondly, the very fact that you have been damaged means you want someone to sweep you off your feet and take care of you. You need someone to say the good things to help you piece your self-esteem back together again. You may have slight reservations at first but you will (and I guarantee you will do this) think, "It can't happen again, I deserve to be happy and he seems so genuine".

Thus you fall straight into my love bomb trap.

How else does this love bombing manifest? We will speak on the telephone for hours at a time. That has never happened with anybody else has it? That shows how special it is. When we meet for dinner you are amazed at how much in common we have. I will send you song titles by text and invite you to look them up on YouTube because the particular song is about you and me. I will find out that you are a keen motorcyclist so I purchase all the necessary items of kit so I can come out on the bike with you. I send excessive gifts (even though often I can ill-afford them), I take you to plush hotels, I introduce you quickly to my coterie of brainwashed admirers who all praise and flatter you. They are just my extensions and lieutenants (more of that below) who amplify my charm.

You think, "What lovely friends he has, he is clearly a delightful and pleasant man." Thus the illusion grows. I will write you poems, leave love notes under your pillow and write your name in a heart in the condensation on the bathroom mirror. Some of my choice phrases include: -

We have so much in common
No one understands me like you do. You get me.
You are my soul mate.
I can't believe I have finally found you
We belong together

I hear you protest, "But these things can happen in a normal relationship, so how do I distinguish between healthy expressions of affection and love-

12

bombing?" It is simple. Yes, all of the things above may happen in a healthy relationship but not after one date and certainly not with the rapidity of a machine gun. Nobody falls in love after three days. (Well they might in the movies, but guess what? They are fictional too). If it is too fast, too often, too outlandish and too grandiose then it is love bombing.

Nothing is off limits for me in this shower of affection. To read more about exactly the types of things that I will say and do in greater detail to love bomb you, read my book **'Evil'**.

How is this love-bombing so effective? There are several reasons: -

- **No time to think**
- **Removal of benign influences**
- **The creation of a false impression**
- **The masking of the truth**
- **Premature establishment of the relationship**
- **Most sought after emotion**

Since it is incessant you are not given any time to think about it. You are not allowed time to reflect on whether it feels right or whether what is being written bears any resemblance to reality. Instead, you are caught up in this whirlwind of romantic intentions and the flattery feels wonderful. You are not given any time to question it and it does not take long before you are hooked on this affection.

The bombardment also takes you away from other people who might be clued into what I am doing and seek to warn you and steer you away from me before my tendrils have actually coiled around you. By being "in your face" all day and every day, nobody will get near enough to you. I will be with you as often as I possibly can in person and then maintain a presence through the texts, calls, emails and social media postings. Hell, if I had a pigeon, he would be carrying messages to you as well.

This carpet-bombing with affection provides you with a false impression of me. I am unable to keep the real me hidden for long, the effort involved is too great and unfortunately there will be occasions when my fuel wanes so that the creature that lurks below will occasionally appear.

You will come to learn that I do not like to expend my energy unnecessarily and want the maximum return for minimal effort. I do not want you to notice negative things such as the fact that my job is not as well paid as I suggest it is or the fact that I have very few friends. Thus, in order to avoid you seeing the abhorrent me too soon, I have to seduce you hard and fast. Hence that is a further reason why my kind and me engage in the love bombing.

This fast and furious technique also drives the relationship forward (often before you are ready) so certain ties are put in place, which bind you to me. For example, I will want to book trips away together and put those in place as soon as possible even though they may be some way off in the future. I will soon start staying over at your house and then I will also look to have us live together after an unfeasibly short period of time. You will not question this however because you are blinded to reality by this technique. If any one tries to caution you about this I will dismiss them as jealous or if my manipulation is taking effect you will disregard what they say because only you know how good it feels to be with me and they do not. You will begin to justify the most ridiculous of scenarios by declaring "It just feels so right with him" or "I know it seems so quick but really we are made for one another, don't you want me to be happy?" You will begin to maintain my own propaganda after a period of time.

We all want to be loved. It is the most sought after trait by humans. Being presented with what is packaged as a perfect love taps deep into your psyche and drives right into your core being. It is almost impossible to resist.

Love bombing is the force majeure of manipulation. It is the opening move and a grand one at that. It is powerful, potent and massively effective. Since it is founded on positive actions, the malevolent intent that lurks behind it is near impossible to detect. It is a key component in my manipulative toolbox and I use it every single time I require fresh fuel.

2. Reflection

I mentioned above that I am highly skilled in the art of reading people, which has arisen from a lifetime of practising the art. This skill is utilised in unleashing the next part of my manipulative portfolio. Reflection. I become an exact mirror of you.

This is effective because I become everything you want. You enjoy ice hockey? Guess what? So do I? Your favourite meal is spaghetti bolognaise. How about that? I love that and even better I have a brilliant recipe for making one. Each thing you like I just happen to like. If you do not enjoy something then neither do I. If you look back you will now think it is odd how we matched on every level. That had never happened with anyone else. Of course, at the time you just told yourself that that was because nobody had been as wonderful as me. You regarded it as a positive thing.

How do I know what to reflect? I follow a three stage process for ensuring I have plenty of material from which to create my mirrors. Firstly, when I first see you (this is usually before we have even spoken) I will do my research about you. I will speak to other people who I know are familiar with you and garner from them as much information as I possibly can. Where you live, other family members, where you work where you went to school and such similar foundations of someone's life.

I then utilise my good friend technology to search on line about you and drill deep into your social media. Look at how many times you post pictures of the meals you make or select when you go to a restaurant? That is why I know you like your steak sanguine and that your enjoy Waldorf salad. I have seen many pictures of you holding a flute of champagne, so I know ordering that drink on a first date will be a winner. You regularly post about the places you have been, the films you have watched and the books you have read. You also post your rants and complaints so I begin to compile a compendium of things you don't like as well.

Secondly, once the love bombing begins I always ensure (initially at least) the conversation is all about you (I know, how ironic) and thus you pour your heart out to me. I have already established what you do, where you live and such like. My research has filled me in on many of your likes and dislikes but this is where I get even more information. Most importantly, I also gather information about your emotions. The people you have been in love with and why. Who has broken your heart (I sit listening with a mask of sympathy rigid on my face as you spill out your guts to me - of course I do not feel any sympathy but I have learned how to show it). You explain to me your family dynamics and which of your colleagues earn your admiration and your contempt. At times I feel like reaching for a notebook when we are together (I do write it all down at the next convenient moment by the way) such is the torrent of brilliant information that you are giving me.

Thirdly, I question and probe by asking lots of questions (aren't I great taking such an interest in you?) and mentioning lots of topics. I watch you very carefully whilst I am doing this. I am probing you. I talk about a certain pop star and I see the corner of your mouth turn down. Okay. You do not like him. I pick another. No, still no good. I move on and then your eyes widen. Bingo! You like her. All three responses are stored away for later use with a note to self that I look up Ellie Goulding's catalogue of records. That way I might find one to use to send you its title by text and furthermore on our next date I can profess to have always been a fan of hers. Who knows? I may just come up with tickets if I perceive your appreciation of her to be high. I continue with our conversation as I watch every movement of your mouth, flaring of your nostrils and dilation of your pupils. I observe where your hands are. I listen to the intonation in your voice when you speak about certain television programmes. I question and probe as I move through the positive and negative cues you provide to me. All the while my encyclopaedia about you is growing larger.

As ever, my manipulation of you in gathering this information serves several purposes - not only am I extracting information from you to allow me to carry out my reflection, I am stockpiling information to use to hurt you later when I engage in Triangulation, Attrition or Threatened Loss.

All of this accumulated knowledge is then used to demonstrate to you that I like what you like and I don't like the same things that you don't like. What does this achieve? Well, it manipulates you into thinking we have a really strong connection. You feel like you have known me for a long time (which in turn helps me accelerate the relationship prematurely as described above). You feel safe with me and encouraged. It feels so very right and what a fantastic start we have made to our new relationship. We have so much in common.

You will be familiar with the phrase "my other half". I know that you are subconsciously seeking your other half, namely someone who mirrors your views, likes, feelings and hopes. I know this is a psychological need in people. You are in essence looking for your doppelganger. In mirroring you I become your other half and thus tap into your deep-seated need to couple with me. My mirroring enables me to ensnare you with greater ease. Moreover, it enables me to forge a strong bond between you and me and draw you completely into my world. Every time you look at me, you will see something of yourself and that will keep you wanting me and fearful of losing me. Of course, it is a complete illusion but you do not know this because my manipulative skill is so good, you are too busy succumbing to the accompanying love bombing whilst telling everybody how wonderful it is that you have found someone who "completes me". You see, there is that other half notion again. Utilising the technique of mirroring is a powerful method of controlling you. Sadly, mirrors have a tendency to shatter, but we are not concerned with that here.

3. Guilt

You will no doubt be aware that much of our emotional outlook on life arises from how we were brought up when we were children. I now know that my childhood has had a significant influence on what I am. I must admit however that I have had my fill of people explaining to me that my behaviour is as a consequence of the way I was treated as a child. However, that discussion has no place here. The fact is that much of how we feel and act as adults, has been shaped from when we were children and that this is a direct link that remains open all our lives. It is a connection between how we felt when we were small and helpless and our adult selves. The highway is clear and direct and certain cues can send us hurtling along it straight back to our formative years.

You may be familiar with the film *Rocknrolla*. In one scene, the actor Mark Strong's character, Archie, is espousing the virtue of a properly administered back-handed slap to a fellow gang member's face. He explains that when done properly, "it transports him right back to childhood". With that, the insinuation is that the stinging chastisement we felt as children when slapped manifests when we are similarly slapped as adults and leave us suitable punished and compliant in the adult moment. Guilt has much the same effect.

I utilise guilt to send you on a trip to childhood. Childhood was full of rules. Do not touch the items in the store. Clear your plate. Say your prayers. Don't make a noise. Wipe your feet before you come in. Every day you had to negotiate more rules and regulations than set down in a statute book. If you failed to do so, then you were rebuked and punished and made to feel guilty for your transgression. This became so imbued in you (as you began your journey to becoming the honest and decent person you are today) that soon the mere threat of feeling guilty ensured you behaved yourself and you did as you were told.

Thus it is deeply ingrained in you that you find guilt particularly shaming and something you wish to avoid as often as you possibly can. I know this about you. I know that because you are an empathic person and you behave with integrity, honesty and decency, that guilt has a particular resonance for you. I then exploit that guilt to further my own aims.

How does this manifest? You may attack me for staying out late when you wanted to spend the evening with me. Indeed, you cooked a delicious meal and bought one of my favourite wines. I was doing what I pleased and was chasing down some fresh supply as I sent my air force to engage in its first sortie of love bombing. When I eventually appear, you are understandably annoyed and thus you launch into an attack. I know you are right but I cannot stand your criticism of me. I absolutely hate being criticised. I must fight back. I must retaliate. There are certain other manipulative techniques I will deploy to deal with what I regard as an unwarranted attack (Denial or Attrition for example) but on this occasion I deploy Guilt.

"I would come home earlier if you made an effort for me. You've gained weight and frankly I find that unappealing. Is it any wonder I don't want to come home and sit with Jabba the Hutt?"

Of course I know that only yesterday you had sighed to yourself that you had gained a few pounds when you were weighing yourself. The reality is you look no different, but I know you feel guilty about that slight weight gain. I am also insinuating that you are selfish by not looking your best for me.

If you were in a healthy situation this would not have been mentioned or even if it had, you would have the critical thinking and awareness to dismiss my remarks as you know it to be untrue (you have not gained any appreciable weight) or it does not matter (it has not affected your appearance) or it is irrelevant (my staying out is nothing to do with how you look). Unfortunately for you, you are not in a healthy relationship and your usual level of self-esteem has been eroded. You instantly feel guilty. You knew you had put weight on. You do look a mess. I am right; if you looked better I would have come back earlier. You are to blame. It is your entire fault.

It can be anything about you that I seize on. Your hair is too short (yesterday it was too long - yes, I will be inconsistent in the blink of an eye), or you dress too sluttish, you never have anything meaningful to say, you didn't buy my favourite cheese and so on. The subject matter is not important so long as I know that it is something you will feel guilty about.

The guilt consumes you and you are taken back to feeling like you are five years old again. The effect creates confusion and paralysis. You can hear one of your parents admonishing you for eating the cake before your dinner and thus ruining your appetite (it never did but when did relevance ever get in the way of admonishment?) and you feel small and helpless. There you stand, defenceless and unable to answer back and you must take your chastisement and learn from it. The learned behaviours of all those years ago surface in an instant. You must not answer back as that will be impertinent. You must apologise and profess your intention to not do it again and that you will behave far better next time. Be better. Think well. Remember for next time. This use of guilt has sent you rushing along the highway to your childhood and your adult self, with all of its rational protecting behaviours has vanished. Now you will act out how you behaved as a naughty, guilt-ridden child. You will stand and apologise, completely forgetting about my poor behaviour as I highlight what you have done wrong by the application of a massive dose of guilt.

4. Intimidation

The champion swimmer Mark Spitz once said

"I believe that the art of winning is through intimidation and not necessarily do you have to speak about it."

Those are wise words indeed.

Intimidation of course is just a fancy way of saying bullying. Intimidation is an interesting technique in manipulation as it relies on the threat of something happening. In order to give that threat weight and credence there needs to have been something happen which strongly suggests that a repeat event may occur or even a more extreme version could happen if you do not do as I want.

I am not one for physical violence. I freely admit that in my rages I could kill but that has a chance of landing me in prison and I do not want that. Whilst I have little doubt I would be the Supreme Being in a prison environment on account of my vastly superior intellect and ever-present charm, I still do not want to spend time there. Physical violence whilst immediate and shocking to the recipient is problematic and if I am to be candid, I view it as more the preserve of the low functioning of our kind. I avoid it for several reasons.

Firstly, it requires the expenditure of energy. Energy, which can be, better directed elsewhere. Secondly, it leaves evidence. In order to operate effectively I need to always maintain plausible deniability (See Denial later) and leaving somebody covered in bruises and cuts tends to rule out plausible deniability, even for someone as skilled as me at telling lies. Thirdly, the use of physical violence can shock the victim into a sudden state of awareness and lifts them out of the altered reality that I have created. This means I run the risk of losing my fuel. It also means I will then have to expend additional energy in either recreating the altered reality (which by now will become even more difficult) or seeking out new fuel. All of this is something that I find irksome. Finally, physical violence will often cause the victim to engage with people outside of my immediate sphere of influence, such as police officers, domestic violence support workers, hospital staff and such like. Whilst one can weave one's magic around them, it does run the risk of outside interference reducing or removing my fuel. Accordingly, I do not engage in serious physical violence.

One has to raise the threat that may occur to keep the intimidation in place and thus the control. I achieve this by breaking things. A plate thrown at the floor or a glass hurled at the wall shows that I am capable of destruction of physical objects and by extension that means I have the capacity to hurt you. Accordingly, that threat generates the intimidation.

I also maintain intimidation by the use of verbal threats. I have threatened an elderly relative with moving them to a less desirable care home. I have raised the spectre of dismissal with subordinate colleagues. I have threatened girlfriends that if they leave I will burn all their clothes. Moreover, those that dared to suggest they would leave I have then reminded of my omnipotence and pointed out how easily I will find it to track their every move, read their e-mails, intercept their messages and watch them from the pavement at night. This intimidation invariably works by causing the recipient to decide to stay. At least then they can see what I am doing and keep an eye on me rather than being alone worrying about what my next move might be.

Intimidation is effective because when I smash that statue that you really like, you want to reduce and eradicate my rage immediately. You will then agree to my terms. I also know that since you exhibit such high amounts of empathy that you will go into a placation mode and seek to appease me by ascertaining what is wrong. This opens the door for me to utilise another form of manipulation, if I so choose, in Attrition.

I use overt threats and I use veiled threats. It all amounts to intimidation, which will then keep you within my control. Veiled threats are especially useful because if you try and involve a third party by complaining about my behaviour, you have two problems. First of all, the person you go to may not see the veiled threat and regard your reaction as paranoia and disproportionate. I always hope this happens as it leads to you receiving a 'crazy' label from that person. In future they will be even less likely to believe you and then eventually they won't believe you, meaning one less person for you to turn to. Secondly, veiled threats are effective yet so easy for me to explain away with my plausible deniability. You may have heard the following phrases

"You are over-reacting"
"You are reading too much into the situation"
"You have a vivid imagination"

These phrases, amongst others, are keystones in demonstrating that you have the problem and that I have done nothing wrong. You, meanwhile, know full well what I meant and therefore you remain concerned for your safety. The intimidation continues and so does the ensuing control.

5. Triangulation

This is a favourite of mine because it is very effective. My kind and me use triangulation repeatedly. It is rolled out very quickly in the devaluation stage. Put simply, I introduce a third party (either a person or sometimes even an object) into our dynamic as a means of manipulating you. It is good for all occasions, be it between lovers, friends, work or family. I have two methods of triangulating. I refer to these as the Traditional Method and the Modern Method.

The Traditional Method is the archetypal introduction of a third person. The Traditional Method can be further split into Real and Imagined. For instance, I am in a relationship with you so I decide to start mentioning a very competent and attractive lady who I work with. I have never mentioned her before. In fact, I have nothing to do with her at all. I see her occasionally enter the building where we both work and assume she works on another floor but I never speak to her and our paths do not cross within work save through the occasional email or being in the same meetings.

Notwithstanding this I make mention of her often to you. I remark how well styled she is, how she has lost weight, that her lips are full and no doubt she is an excellent kisser. I remark on how diligent she is and that she was awarded a bonus. I identify any trait of hers that I know you will be sensitive about (you don't dress up very often, you've gained weight, your lips are thin, you are not currently working and so on). I have created an Imagined Competitor for you and thus the triangulation has begun. This eats away at you because I am pressing exactly the right buttons to provoke you but you run the risk of any complaints you issue being dismissed by reasonable of plausible deniability. Over dinner I have mentioned her several times and you say,

"You seem to mention Trisha a lot, is there something I should know?"

I stop eating and lower my fork. I fix you with a cold stare and then an empty smile.

"Well of course I mention her a lot we are working on the same project at present."
"You don't mention anyone else from the project."
"Do I not? I think you will find I do (**denial**) but you seem to have developed an obsession about Trisha (**blame shift**). Of course, her excellence at work makes her stand out (**reinforcement of original sleight**). Am I not allowed to praise my colleagues now? (**provocation**)"
"Yes but you keep mentioning her."
"I think you are over-reacting. Are you jealous because I talk to a colleague?"
"Well no, but,"
"This is typical of you. I go to work and work hard all day. I come home and share my work with you and you immediately find a reason to criticise me about it. I tell you what, how about I don't talk to you about work? How about I give up work? How would you like that? Do you want to live in a tiny flat on welfare because I can just do that if that's what you would prefer?"
Cue my indignant rage and you immediately trying to soothe me, apologising and backing down. My dominance is asserted and once again you are made out to be the bad person. This is all logged in my mind as well (see the later chapter on Bringing Up the Past).
Accordingly, I have provoked a reaction from you, made you anxious and asserted my control over you all through the fictitious mention of another lady at work.

That was the Imagine version. Naturally, in the Real version I am actually interacting with that person and I am probably engaged in an affair with that person. I speak highly of her so that you are provoked into action. You do not want to lose me so you redouble your efforts to please me. Meanwhile, I am securing fuel from my new conquest that I am subjecting to a campaign of love bombing. It is coming at me from two directions and I am revelling in it. In the Traditional Method where I am triangulating with someone else I will invariably switch the roles around at some point, so that I start to pay you more attention and tell you that the affair is over. Meanwhile, I still continue the affair but I am telling Trisha that I am considering staying with you, so she increases her efforts to keep me. I will vacillate back and forth in this manner. One of you will be the perpetrator making my life a (supposed) misery and the other my rescuer with me always as the victim. Your roles swap and mine stays the same. It is very effective.

The added bonus is that you won't blame me but you will blame the third party. She is the one ruining the relationship and you want to tackle her. I can sit back with my hands behind my head and a broad smile on my face as I watch you two fight over me and engage in providing me with an ego feeding frenzy. You would think that both of you would turn on me but that does not happen. You both want me and think that the other is obstructing your relationship with me. You may find that surprising but this is what happens because that is how effective my manipulation through triangulation is.

I also made reference to the Modern Method of triangulation. This is where I introduce an inanimate object into the dynamic of our relationship. You may read that and wonder how that works. By way of example, I may purchase a new car. I am proud of the vehicle and I am always talking about how fast it will go, how responsive the steering is and how it clings to the road. I repeatedly discuss the places I go to in my new car. I spend hours cleaning it and polishing it. I sometimes just sit inside of it, drinking in that gorgeous new car scent. Are you starting to see a familiar pattern now? I lavish attention on the car and not on you. You cannot accuse me of having an affair with a car but its involvement in our relationship irks you and provokes a reaction from you. You will complain about how I think more of the car than you, that it goes to better places than I take you to and that I spend more on the car than I do on you. Cue my plausible deniability and my amazed indignation as I declare,

"Are you seriously jealous of a car. You need help."

Job is done.

My absolute favourite use of the Modern Method is triangulating you with my mobile phone. I sit fiddling with it when we are together or it is shoved away in my jacket but you can hear it bleeping and ringing. Who is trying to contact me? It then vanishes for days on end as I have hidden it somewhere. You try and call me but there is no answer and I trot out the excuses.

"There was no signal in the area."
"There is a problem with my phone."
"You left a voicemail? It must not be working as I did not pick one up."
"I could not call as I ran out of credit."
"The texts don't seem to be sending/receiving."

All of this is designed to annoy you and provoke a reaction from you. It is very successful.

Triangulation is a master manipulative technique for ensuring I receive my fuel. It keeps you in a state of anxiety, provokes reactions and allows me in certain scenarios to receive double the fuel that I might ordinarily harvest.

6. Lieutenants

I ensure that I have a coterie of faithful followers. They can be drawn from any background. Sometimes they are colleagues (they work best as they like to engage in sycophancy in the hope of securing a promotion). Other times they are a small number of friends I have known a long-time and who have become completely inured to my way of thinking that they are little more than automatons. Alternatively they will be comprised of family members who believe the sun shines from my backside. The way that these lieutenants are constituted can alter from time to time but what does remain the same is that I have my Praetorian guard, which will support me and question you. Always.

In the early stages of devaluation you will predictably seek validation from someone else that my behaviour is out of order and that you are not the one who is acting incorrectly. This is a standard response and one, which I rely on and prepare for. I often hear the threat from you that you will speak to my best friend and tell them just what I really am or that you are ringing your parents so they know just how golden boy really treats his girlfriend. It is all I can do to prevent myself from laughing. I invite you to do it and watch as you founder on their impenetrable support of my status quo.

These people are my loyal supporters. Whoever goes running to them is regarded as a telltale and in possession of 'the crazy'. They will actually listen to you thus allowing you to think that they are considering what you are saying before they will politely explain to you how you are mistaken. You will try again and they will repeat the process, sometimes roping in other lieutenants so that the impenetrable wall remains intact. You begin to doubt yourself since after all, these people have known me a lot longer than you have. Their explanations are convincing and seem logical (after all they have had a lot of practice doing this explaining) and you slink away confused and beaten.

If you persist they will turn on you and label you as hysterical and suggest that it is you that has the problem. Sound familiar? They have all been well trained by me. I ensure that well before you go running to them I have subjected you to a Character Assassination so that if they had the slightest doubt that this time you are in the right, my insidious whisperings about you soon put paid to any shred of credibility that you once had. The more you protest the more, in their eyes, you are fulfilling precisely what I said you would do.

I will even look to recruit my lieutenants from amongst your family and friends. I do this when I am in the love bombing stage and they see the decency oozing from me so that they all conclude I am an honest and upright individual and aren't you lucky to have met me? You of course have been telling them this from day one as well so they do not need much convincing from me to swallow my propaganda. You become the architect of your own downfall.

I create some Kafkaesque nightmare where you dash from person to person plaintively declaring,

"It's not me, it is him, and he is the problem."

Unfortunately for you, you are met with shakes of the head, tuts and mutterings of "poor girl, she has got herself in a state over nothing again."

My lieutenants are arranged to cover all the various facets of our lives where you might seek help. They are utterly loyal, cannot be persuaded of anything other than to support me. You will be left banging your head on the proverbial brick wall. This is manipulation by proxy and it is particularly satisfying.

7. Obsessing

With the manipulative tactic of obsessing I have you doing most of the work for this. This is naturally a bonus for me as I get to save energy. With a combination of other techniques, I generate a heightened state of anxiety for you. I have created a false reality and plunged you right into the middle of it. I say certain things and take certain steps, all coated with some trusty plausible deniability. This has the effect of causing you to obsess over our relationship. You begin to over analyse every conversation that we have, scrutinising the meaning and considering the tone in which I spoke. You read something into every syllable and search for understanding from my responses. Even the way I said 'hello' is placed under the microscope.

You assume the role of detective as you try and work out what is really going on in our relationship. In time-honoured fashion, you are so busy looking for a meaning that you miss precisely what is right in front of you. You become fixated on trying to solve the problem but you are looking in the wrong place.

You ruminate over the way I looked at you. What did he mean by that glance? What was behind his comment that he was busy today? Busy doing what? Why did he not say? Is there some agenda to him suddenly becoming busy? When I rang his 'phone it went on to voicemail. Has he switched his phone off? Maybe he has no signal, but he is in the city today, he told me that. Maybe he was lying? Then again he might have been on another call. Who was that to and if his 'phone was on, he must have seen he had a missed call from me but an hour has passed and he has not returned my call. Often there will be an entirely innocent explanation behind this and I could easily provide it to you to ease your concerns. I choose not to. I want you trying to work things out. I want you sat trying to figure out what is going on. I know you are unsure of what to do as you try to do the right thing.

You are sat wondering what I am thinking. You decide that you would not do what I have done so this leads you to ask why have I done it? What does it mean? If you had done it, you would think it means A but I did say it meant B, but that was last month. What if I have changed now and it means C? Round and round you go. You sit and stew and ferment and I know that you won't actually do anything. You will be paralysed by your own indecision. You want all the answers but you do not realise you cannot have them. You certainly cannot have them when you are dealing with someone like me. I take refuge in the uncertain. I move in and out of the shadows. Ambiguity follows me everywhere and I play upon it to ensure that your obsessive nature is given every chance to appear.

As usual, in the early stages of our blossoming relationship I will have worked out that you are short on confidence and not someone who makes decisions quickly or firmly. I seize on that. I know that you like to consider something from every conceivable angle and then do it all again. You derive a curious perverted enjoyment from scrutinising everything in our relationship. You are a prime candidate for me behaving in a vague and amorphous way so that the Obsessing card is played.

The consequence of your obsessing is such that you are being manipulated. You are putting yourself into a state of anxiety and worrying about matters over which you have little control. Sustaining this heightened state is very draining. It is akin to having a diminished battery in a car and putting the headlamps on full beam. You soon find the windscreen wipers are moving slowly and the radio won't work. By investing too much energy in obsessing, your anxious state means you are left with less to defend yourself when I unleash a different form of manipulation. Accordingly, moving you into this obsessive state is a great way of softening you up.

In addition, the fact I know you are obsessing in such detail means that I am well and truly slap bang in the middle of your thoughts. That makes me feel powerful. I know you are thinking about me over and over. You are letting me rent space in your head and you are not even charging me for it. This provides me with further fuel.

I would wager good money you are now obsessing about whether everything I have written is applicable to your partner. Go on, chew it over for a few years, you know you want to.

8. Promised Gains

During the love bombing seduction phase I created what you regard as our golden period. Everything was wonderful. Addictive memories that you repeatedly play through your mind were created during those halcyon days. It was an exciting time it was uplifting and mesmerising. I told you things that nobody had ever said to you before. I took you to wonderful places, made love to you often and with magnificent passion that surpassed any love that you had before. Every day felt like Christmas Day as I surprised you with more and more love, warmth, affection and desire. The gifts arrived, the texts bombarded and the seduction oozed around you. It was unique.

And yet like every shining empire that has ever existed it all came crashing down. The affection dried up, I stopped making love to you or if I did it was mechanical and robotic. I rarely wanted to do anything together anymore. I preferred to spend my days connected to an Xbox or watching sport endlessly on television (Modern Method Triangulation anyone?). I started to disappear and you could not get hold of me. I mentioned other women and you began to wonder if I was playing away. I started to criticise you for the very things I once said I adored you for. The world felt cold and a forlorn wind blew through bare trees where once sweet blossom fell about us as we kissed. I have you firmly in the stage of devaluation.

It is during this stage that the technique of Promised Gains is used. I have two ways of utilising this. The first is opening the door on heaven again and allowing you to feel the heady warmth of that glorious sunshine once more, but only for a short while. I surprise you and take you away for the weekend and it feels like how things used to be. I remember a particular picture you like and purchase it for you, hanging it in the bedroom and you are reduced to tears, borne out of joy and relief because the man you fell in love with has returned.

You knew it. You knew I would come back to you. That is why you hung in there. That is why you clung on tight despite all the insults I hurled at you. You knew that things would come good again and they have. The effect of me opening the door to heaven again is intoxicating for you. Not only does it feel so wonderful to experience my brilliant affection again (just like a drug addict finally scoring a hit once more) but also the relief you feel from the misery you have been put through during the devaluation is immense. The doubts are cast aside and you wholeheartedly embrace this return. Of course it does not last. I slam the door shut after a few days (most likely disappearing for a while into the bargain) and you are cast down from that heaven and plummet back into hell again.

Only this time you have been manipulated to think that you can get that door back open again. It has happened once hasn't it? Accordingly, you convince yourself based on the very fact that you witnessed it that if you hang in there, please me, ensure I am not irritated by you and that you succumb to my every whim and diktat you will be able to return to the heaven of the golden period. This time you will get it right so you remain there. It is so addictive that you commit all of your dwindling resources to achieving this; utterly oblivious to the fact I did this on purpose to ensure your ultimate compliance. The promise of heaven will see you do anything to please me. Talk about a fuel injection.

The second way that I utilise the technique of Promised Gains is to keep telling you that something good is going to happen. Yes we will have that week away you keep mentioning. It will be marvellous. I am just rather busy at present but as soon as I have a moment I promise you that I will book the holiday. I may take this one step further and promise you that I will change my ways. I know I have a violent temper. I am sorry I shout at you. Yes, I will see someone about anger management. I want to change for you. I will do it, I promise, I am just not ready yet. I often deploy this particular brand of Promised Gain if I sense there is a risk that you might leave me. It is sufficiently powerful to bring you back into the fold.

I manage to string you along with these promises on which I will never deliver. Your coping mechanisms have been worn away by my repeated manipulation so that you fail to see that in fact months or even years have passed and nothing has changed. I have not delivered on the promise. I have not done what I said I would do. I continue to promise jam tomorrow and so fearful are you of losing out on that promised nirvana you trudge along sustained on the scintilla of an empty promise, craving that dollop of sweet, sweet jam.

9 Threatened Loss

This form of manipulation is a sugar coated knuckle-duster. The way I utilise this is to make you concerned that you will lose me. Keep in mind that I have Love Bombed you and subjected you to a golden period, which is a powerful and addictive tool for ensuring you remain invested in the relationship or invested in the expectation that the relationship will return to that state. I will say certain things, which are threats that you will lose me and this is designed to control you.

The chief way in which I will do this is to use this phrase,

"I love you, but."

Love is the most powerful emotion. Nearly everybody wants to be loved or for you to love something of theirs. Chefs want diners to love their meals, artists want people to love their creations and companies want customers to love their products. It is surprising how love, since it is bandied around so much, has never lost any of its potency. That in itself is testament to how powerful it is.

When my sentence begins with I love you, you feel that heady warmth rising and that sense of delight at those three words. It also masks the true intent of what I am saying. For instance, if I say to you,

"I love you but I wish you would not wear that dress,"

I am sending a criticism your way by suggesting that you dress in an inappropriate manner. I keep making these comments and they are like a jab from a boxer, weakening you and designed to whittle away at your self-esteem and confidence. Furthermore, the use of "I love you, but" carries with it the threat that I will take away that love. You are desperate to avoid that happening and the spectre of a threatened loss induces a compliant response in you.

However, because of the way I have conditioned you, you will hear my sentence and not regard it as a criticism. You will think that I care about how you look and that you are lucky to have someone who is interested in your appearance. The outcome remains the same. You don't want to lose me because you fear that is what might happen and you also have that fear reinforced by my backhanded compliment. Accordingly, you will go and change your attire to something, which meets with my approval. Threatened loss is a particularly covert method of achieving an effective manipulation of you.

10. Attrition

Commentators refer to a war of attrition whereby both sides wear one another down. That is not the definition applicable here. This tactic wears down only one side and that side is you. Although a number of the manipulative techniques do have the effect of reducing your self-esteem, lowering your guard and dismantling your critical thinking those consequences are not the primary aim of this technique. In this instance, the main aim is to wear you down.

    This is done by a steady drip drip drip approach. I chip away at your resolve with an unpleasant comment here and a malign act there. One day I might throw away a small trinket in which you place great sentimental value. On another day I criticise what you wear or how you have done your hair. I aim to demean, belittle and denigrate. Anything and everything about your life and how you lead it comes into my sights. I see you pouring a glass of wine; you are drinking too much. I hear you laughing; be quiet, I am trying to watch a television programme. I start small to begin with so that you feel a degree of mild irritation at my comment. You may think that you have hidden your reaction, however slight it might be, from me. Remember, I am highly skilled at reading you and I will of course be looking out for a reaction however innocently I may dress up my remark. Over time I continue to ratchet up the level of denigration so that my criticism becomes more often and more biting. They also become ridiculous.

    On Monday you asked me what I wanted for dinner the next evening and I explained I wanted steak. On Tuesday you cooked the steak and I sit and eat it all before remarking that that was not what I wanted. You are staggered. You know I asked for steak because that is why you went and bought it. You have also just watched me eat it. I fix you with one of my cold stares daring you to challenge me. You remain silent. I press on and say that not only was it not what I wanted but you did not cook it properly. I know you pride yourself on your culinary skills (and with good reason) so I choose an assault that addresses something where you feel strong. My comments increase as I widen the criticism to encompass all the meals you make, the times you make them and how much it is costing (leaving aside the issue that you pay half the food bill). Before you can respond I make myself scarce and then reappear later as if nothing has been said. However, the demeaning observations are still festering with you.

At the next mealtime I pick up where I left off and find something else to have a go at you about. I criticise your choice of seasoning or the vegetables that you served. I contradict myself repeatedly but I do not care as I keep pushing and prodding. I know you hate confrontations and therefore you will do anything to avoid me exploding into a rage so you nod and placate as I continue with my litany of baseless brickbats.

I shift tack and begin to debase your efforts at work. I comment on how late you keep arriving home and how you are neglecting domestic duties. Still you will not react because you know what happens if you do. The days become a week and then a month and still my chipping away continues. I make a snide remark about your shoes and then a hostile comment about your friends. I can see how it is troubling you and how you are becoming wearisome of my incessant adverse observations about you.

I keep the pot simmering, just doing sufficient to niggle you but not enough to cause an explosion. I am very good at this. Like Chinese water torture my lack of appreciation and repeated put downs press upon you. You are miserable. You are tired of hearing them and you are dying to erupt but you won't as my reaction will be far worse and you cannot stand for that to happen.

Eventually, so worn down are you, that you will begin to second-guess what I want. You will not do anything without first considering the implications. I have seen you jotting down what I have said so you can refer back to it to ensure that you do the right thing, record the right television programme and purchase the correct brand of chilli sauce. When you get it right I either say nothing or pluck out some criticism. I can see your will eroding and your identity slipping away as you start to look at the world through my eyes, saying what I want to hear and becoming little more than an automaton. It is one for the long haul and works best with those who are blessed with considerable patience and a reluctance to confront, but applying attrition brings you under my eventual control. It is steady and insidious and devastatingly effective.

11.   Character Assassination

Although this is similar to Attrition in that it is an attack on you and what you do, this is both direct and indirect as well as being far more savage. I go for the jugular when I am with you and I engage in a concentrated smear campaign behind your back. The gloves are off and it is open season when I decide to deploy Character Assassination.

What lies behind my use of character assassination? Two things. Those things are envy and the desire to manipulate. Why envy? I don't have a real identity, I always look to borrow the identity of others and subsume it within me. That means that I take on the traits and interests and others although I do not truly understand how it feels to be that person. By way of example, let's say that you enjoy watching football (soccer). You go every weekend to the stadium and enjoy discussing the team selection with your friends and other supporters. You reflect on the previous result, analyse the opposition and consider how the game will go. You kick every ball with the players, you feel the elation when your team scores, you sink into your seat when your team concedes a goal. Indignation arises at a poor refereeing decision, which goes against your team. You can taste the tea from the concession stand; smell the hot dogs and pies that are on sale. There is that electric buzz of a large crowd being together causing the hairs to stand up on your neck when the crowd chants as one. You identify with all of this (you have told me all about these sensations that's how I know about them). I decide I like going to football matches too but I don't relate to all those feelings that you describe. I am detached from it as I am just borrowing the love of football to say that I do. I do not feel it. That is how I am with most things that I call as my own. I do not relate to them.

Since I cannot relate to them, I become envious. I see that they bring you happiness, excitement and joy but I cannot feel those things. I see you are placed in a good mood by attending the football (or anything else that you engage in) and I hate the fact you can derive joy from it when I cannot. Thus my envy rises.

I cannot control my envy and the only way I know how to deal with it, is to devalue the thing I envy. Continuing the football analogy, I make snide remarks about your team's performance in order to belittle the thing you enjoy. I take delight when your team loses and I see it upsets you. I repeatedly suggest the stadium is decrepit, the services there are rubbish and that the pitch is a disgrace. I barrack the centre forward who you worship and I pour scorn on your devotion to your team. It could be anything you like and thus that I envy. I will attack it.

Once I have begun attacking the item I envy that is associated with you, my envy grows so I become envious of you as a person. Thus my attacks shift onto you and I make the horrible remarks about your appearance, what you say, what you do, whom you socialise with and where you go. My remarks are caustic, bitter and savage. Often I leave you in tears as I launch into another vitriolic tirade. I often combine this manipulative technique with that of Projection (see below).

Not only do I engage in a Character Assassination to your face but also I roll out its nasty sister the Smear Campaign. I will go around telling as many people as I can find all about your unreasonable behaviour. I explain to them how you never let me go out without it being a battle first and how you only ever think of yourself. I give fictional examples of when I have been waiting for you to come in and you eventually appear at 3am, drunk and abusive after whoring yourself around.

I embark on this Character Assassination of you to others behind your back and prior to discarding you. Later on when you try and complain about my behaviour to these people, they regard you suspiciously and you can almost hear the whispers of "he did say she was crazy" because I have got in first and polluted their minds with my toxic words. They just look at you and meet you with silence because I have done such a perfect job in slandering you to them. Of course, because I know all about you and especially your weaknesses, I open up my stockpile of stored facts about you and throw them around town. I snicker as I tell your colleagues about how many times you have wet the bed when you have been drunk. I mention to your keep fit group attendees that you are terrified of spiders and call the police when you see one so they take the arachnid away. I remember all your concerns and weaknesses and now show them to the world as I figuratively plunge the knife in again and again to your character.

When I do this to your face, it makes me feel powerful and reinforces my superiority over you. Usually it will cause you to back down and feel vulnerable so you will look for some way to placate me and thus provide me with fuel. This manipulation of you enables me to maintain my control over you. Deploying this to the wider community ensures that I continue to exert a control over you, even when I have discarded you. You try and rail against my smear and convince people that I was the one in the wrong and it was not you. Word comes back to me that you are talking about me and as you know I love nothing more that ensuring that you are giving me attention be it to my face or by talking about me. It also tells me that I remain very much in your thoughts and along with Obsessing that pleases me. I need to know that my influence lives on in your life even if I have cast you aside. It also enables me to know that should I wish to re-engage with you, it should present no difficulty as I am still very much wired into your psyche.

Most assassins are graceful and never seen. There is nothing hidden or graceful about the way I will assassinate your character. It is brutal and unmerciful.

12. Denial

Denial is a necessary mechanism. It is necessary for healthy people as a defence mechanism. It is necessary for me as a manipulative technique. For you, an obvious example would be the death of a loved one. You are overwhelmed by this loss. In order to protect your mind in the light of this emotional shock, you may go into a state of denial, namely you deny that your spouse or mother has died. This enables you to cope with the shock of the event until your mind is able to then deal with the loss.

Do not make the mistake of thinking that when I deny something it is because deep down I am in pain as a consequence of my behaviour and similar to the example above, I am denying the behaviour to try and deal with the pain. This is incorrect. I am not in pain as a result of what I have done. I do not regard whatever act it is I have committed, as something that is bad, hence there is no pain.

Instead, when I use denial it enables me to manipulate you to achieve several outcomes: -

- You give up your attack against me
- I make you feel bad for attacking me
- I continue to do what I want

I will lie and deny that I have done anything wrong. I will keep on denying it. I will repeatedly deny what you are accusing me of and I will keep going. I should have been a politician such is my ability to deny what is right in front of me. My shutters down and stonewall defence is impregnable. It becomes wearing for you to keep repeating your accusation against me. In the end you will become fed up and just stop. Accordingly, I have defeated your attack against me without any admission of wrongdoing or accountability on my part.

The insistence of my denials then has the effect of making you feel like you have done something wrong. You have failed to show that I have been guilty of what you have accused me of. You are accordingly prejudicial, unfair, judgemental and hectoring. I will happily make those points for you by allying Denial with Projection. At the end of the discussion (I use that term in its most elastic sense) you have failed in your attack and now I have made you feel bad.

Moreover, your failure to achieve an outcome, which results in an admission by me, means that I have not accepted what I did, was wrong. Nor have you been able to prove what I did was wrong. I regard that as validation that what I had done was permissible and acceptable, clearing the way for me to go and do it again.

I deploy differing techniques of denial. I will usually flatly deny that what has happened actually did happen. This is where I like to unveil my very good friend, plausible deniability. I can sense when you have some doubt and I will drive a truck filled with uncertainty through that chink of doubt in order to blow apart your accusations. Alternatively, I will question your recall of the event. Again, when I scent a degree of confusion on your part I will seize on it and hammer home the message that you have got it wrong. This becomes more and more useful since the more you start to doubt yourself, the more often I will exploit this and I will also remind you of your previous memory failings in a bid to convince you that once again you are incorrect.

Try and refer to someone else to support your castigation of me and I will avoid that too. If somehow you have avoided speaking to one of my Lieutenants and instead you have enlisted the support of someone untouched by my corrupting charm, I will deny they are entitled to sit in judgement of me.

"Oh Louise says I did it did she? Well she would. You know she is jealous that you and me are together. Did you not know that? (Why not throw in some Triangulation too) Yes, she has been after me for ages. I am surprised you haven't noticed. She is just doing this to try and split us up. Do you want her to do that?"

Thus, I deny that Louse has any valid basis for supporting your criticism and she is denied as evidence in your case against me.

A different way for me to deny the validity of what you are saying is to compare my behaviour to something worse (wait, someone behaves worse than me?). You criticise me for forgetting an anniversary when you have remembered it. I cannot deny that this has happened so I will again attack the validation of your standpoint in a similar fashion to the above. However on this occasion I will seek to remove your validity by trivialising your complaint.

"Oh have you heard yourself? It is just an anniversary. It wasn't even an important one. It was only three years. Good grief, it's not as if someone has died is it? You are carrying on as if there has been a mass murder of your family. You need to get some perspective."

I will follow this up with some choice observations such as

" You are too sensitive"

"You are always on my case"

"It wasn't that bad"

"You are making a mountain out of a molehill. Again."

One of my favourite retorts when you are seeking to blame me or you are trying to get me to admit I have done something wrong is to say,

"That's just the way I am, deal with it." ;
"I can't help it"
"It was just an impulsive act; you know what I am like."

Once again this statement is a denial of the gravity of my poor behaviour. Instead I am suggesting it is normal for me (ironically it is - did I just tell the truth there?) but what this statement does is shift the footing of your attack. I make it appear that you are no longer attacking the act or the event but you are actually assaulting me as a whole. You are cutting me down. With a deft move to Projection I am able to reinforce my denial.

If you are getting a bit smart and provide me with some evidence of my wrongdoing, for example a text or a recording, I will claim it is out of context. If that is not working, I will then deny the standpoint you are doing. Yes, you might very well have caught me flirting with our neighbour again and you have filmed it and played it back to me, but there is nothing wrong with me talking to someone is there? I cannot deny the act but I can deny the connotation you attach to it. After all, one person's flirting is another person's friendliness surely?

My final act of denial is just to walk away. I am no longer even admitting that the conversation is happening and thus I can deny its contents. The step of walking off and making myself unavailable is a two-pronged denial move. It is a powerful and in effect a cut-off of the conversation. My denial is so great I can just leave. It also denies you any further opportunity to continue to harangue me. I deny the issue and you are denied the chance to air the issue.

Ultimately, however, you face one huge problem. My use of denial is set in stone and will always be used and cannot be defeated. There is a straightforward reason for this. In my mind I always minimise the impact of what I have done. I trivialise it and regard it as de minimis. I then rationalise that what I did was actually required and was justified. Since I deny to myself that I have done anything wrong, how on earth can I ever admit it to you? My denials to you are predicated on my internal denial to myself. That is why I can keep denying and denying and denying. You are dealing with an immovable force.

Denial is powerful. It has a deep-seated basis in my make-up and cannot be defeated. I will use it in several different ways to prevent you from being able to criticise me and then use it once again to further my own agenda against you.

13. Projection

Number thirteen is projection. Unlucky for some. Unlucky for you. Everybody projects although most people do it unwittingly and with no real consequence. My kind and me do it intentionally and we do so for a multiplicity of reasons.

What is happening here is that I see my own unacceptable behaviour and desires in other people. I put that behaviour there so it no longer becomes my behaviour and desire but I see them as belonging to someone else and thus I am absolved of any responsibility for them. I also do this so I can feel superior. You have the unpleasant behaviour, not me and accordingly, I am superior to you.

Projection serves both as a defence mechanism for me and a method of control concerning you. I know the awful behaviours I engage in and I also am fully aware of my real, damaged self. This terrible reality slams into me either as a consequence of you telling me the truth of what I have done or periodically I have a terrifying moment of self-realisation and it hurts. This usually stems from criticism, which I hate.

The pain I feel when I am given a dose of this reality from time to time is overwhelming. Rather than try to change how I behave so this pain might be relieved or be permanently erased, I need something to provide me with a quick fix to get rid of it. The answer is projection. I immediately accuse you of the very thing I am or the very thing that I have done. You are the dishonest one, you are telling lies, you do not show any consideration towards me and you are the one chasing other people outside of our relationship. It is you that forgot the correct birthday present or you messed up the work presentation. I am wired to do this projection automatically. I do it without thinking and I truly believe what I am saying is correct. I have to be convinced of this for it to work.

Whether it has been triggered by your comment to me or a sliver of self-realisation, I have to remove the agony I feel rapidly. Therefore you are told that you are the problem, you are hysterical and you are selfish. I immediately feel relieved of the behaviour and the pain vanishes (but only for now).

This is also done to afford me control of you. By projecting my behaviour onto you, I am reinforcing that you have low self-esteem. I must reinforce that message to you and thus this gives me greater control over you. Attacking you in this fashion enables me to shift from feeling hurt and in pain to feeling empowered once again. That is why projection is so useful to me and why it happens automatically.

The sheer scale of my accusations against you when it is blatantly obvious that I am the one in the wrong will leave you stunned. I will always engage in this behaviour. If in court the judge criticises me for not copying in my opponent and say an independent expert with a piece of correspondence or a witness statement. I will project. I should have copied them in, but I am being criticised and therefore I will retort by stating,

"I don't receive copies of documents from them."

There is absolutely no basis in this comment. They have always copied me in. Someone healthy might respond by saying,

"I am sorry I forgot" or "I didn't realise I had to, I will do it next time."

I will not. I immediately project my failing by accusing the other party in the case and the expert of doing the very thing I have not done even though it is a complete fabrication. It is an aggressive default setting. I am a projection machine such is the immediacy and regularity by which I utilise this technique.

The deployment of this tactic is also particularly wearing for you. You will tire of hearing me trot out the same responses (because you have to keep pointing out to me the same transgressions that I repeat time and time again). This will, like many of my manipulative techniques wear you down so that in the end you will cease to argue with me about it. You are then handing me control by validating the behaviour by no longer criticising it.

You will probably be aware enough to realise that I am labelling you with the horrible actions that I commit although you will not have realised that I am projecting onto you. Instead, you will be flabbergasted by the rank hypocrisy that I am exhibiting. I know I am being a hypocrite and I am doing it on purpose. In part is for the reasons detailed above but it is also because I know you are aware I am being a hypocrite and I want to provoke a reaction from you. You will find it very hard not to react to the appearance of my hypocrisy as you will see it as a shot at an open goal You will be surprised that I have left myself wide open to such an opportunity. What you do not know is that I have done this on purpose and done this so that you will react and react strongly. This will give me more attention and thus more fuel. It is also likely to cause you to erupt and therefore I can label you as histrionic, unstable and crazy. This provides me with some useful materials to use in other forms of manipulation (see Character Assassination). You see how smart I am. I have it all worked out.

14. Reading You

I have alluded earlier to my ability to read you and how that assists me in the Love Bombing phase so I can elicit your likes and dislikes. I am, through repeated practice, an expert in the art of reading people and especially body language. I am a keen student of how people act so that this gives away what they are thinking. Whilst my act of reading you is not itself an act of manipulation, I use the knowledge that I acquire in doing this for my own malign purposes and subsequent manipulation of you. I therefore take the view that it merits inclusion.

When I am closing in on a female target for the purposes of opening up my love bombing, I need to ensure that she is interested and thus susceptible to the forthcoming manipulation. In our opening exchange I am not paying much attention to what she is saying but instead to what she is doing. I am looking for such acts as the head toss and the exposure of her wrists. The smooth soft skin of your wrists is an erotic area of your body and if you show your wrists to me then I know you are interested. Interestingly, homosexual males also make use of the head toss and exposed wrists, so the homosexual of our kind will be on the look out for those gestures also.

I pay special attention to your legs. If your knee is pointing my way then you are signalling interest to me. If I observe that you are fondling your shoe, you are evidently relaxed in my presence and if you go so far as to keep putting your foot in and out of your shoe then I know what you are subconsciously thinking with that movement. Your mouth merits analysis also. I know I am on to a winner when you start applying more make up, as you want to appear more attractive to me, but you are also mimicking what is happening elsewhere in your body. Your state of arousal is leading to blood rushing to your breasts and genitals and therefore by adding make-up you are signalling to me what is going on beneath your clothes.

In larger gatherings where perhaps I am looking to single you out from a crowd so I can make you the object of my attention, I apply these techniques too. Are you standing in a public zone, thereby showing little interest or have you moved into the personal or even intimate zones? If you have, then I know you are interested and I can move in for the kill. If I observe that you have your thumbs tucked into your belt or the top of your trousers then I have hit the jackpot as this sexually aggressive stance on your part is a definite green light (although I am careful to ensure other cues if I happen to be at a line dancing convention or a hoe down).

Not only I am aware of indicators that show your interest I am aware of those latent signals, which show I may have my work cut out, or I should not even waste my time in trying to ensnare you. I always look to see where your feet are pointing. Yes you may be looking at me and smiling but your feet are pointing away from me indicating you want to get away. I usually move on when I see this, as there will be someone else far easier to trap, rather than wasting precious energy trying to bring you around.

I also use these cues to know if I am getting to you when applying another technique of manipulation. If I observe you rubbing the back of your neck, I know that my antagonism is working since you are signalling that I am a pain in the neck, by rubbing yours. If I see a man pulling at his collar I know that he telling me a lie since his neck is warming as a consequence of the lie and he wishes to alleviate the discomfort by tugging on his collar.

There are scores of visual cues that I can take from the way you move, act, sit and stand. I have studied them for years and I make considerable use of them to understand how you are feeling so I then know best what to do or say next.

15. Silence

That was just my little joke. I wonder if that silent, empty page started to imbue the same sensation in you that my use of silence as a manipulative tool does in others? People often use silence. The pregnant pause in a speech to emphasise a point. The silent denouement is used at the end of a play to convey the effect of the powerful final soliloquy that has just been spoken. You will find silence is utilised through out life in order to bring about a response. I am little different. I use silence to bring about a response. I want to get from you a response, which is an emotional response.

I remember speaking to a management consultant and he explained that at the end of his presentations he does not say anything. He waits and waits until those listening speak. He explained he wanted them to set the agenda of the discussion and provoke them into talking to him. Silence is a powerful device.

When I first subject you to the silent treatment the effect on you is devastating. You repeatedly try to contact me and speak to me to find out what is wrong. What has caused this sudden dropping of the shutters when only the day before we were lying in bed together as I told you how I was so pleased to have finally found the one? Your need to know is so great that it completely overrides any sense of embarrassment or decorum on your part. You call my mobile phone again and again and again. You call my work phone repeatedly but find my secretary (one of my loyal lieutenants) will block you by explaining every time you telephone that I am in a meeting. You will call around at my house. I can see you through a gap in the blinds as you hammer on the door and then pace backwards and forwards, frustration and confusion writ large on your face. The text messages pile up. My email inbox begins to bulge and you start shoving letters through my letterbox. I do actually read them as they give me a magnificent sense of importance as I read your questions.

Inevitably the tenor of your attempts to contact me alters. From starting with questions such as "What is wrong?" and "Is something the matter?" you then begin to examine yourself. You query what you might have done to upset me and cause this cessation of communication. Without fail, every time I have deployed this weapon, you have scrutinised yourself to such a degree that you eventually find something that could have caused my reaction. You do this, demeaning yourself, because you need to have an answer as to why this has happened. You must. If you cannot get an answer from me then you turn on yourself and find it there.

"I'm sorry I didn't cook your steak the way you like it" or "I'm sorry I left without kissing you" or "I'm sorry I used the last of the milk and did not replace it". Then come the promises to make things up to me if I will just get in touch. You issue promises stating that you won't do it again and you will be a better person (you are starting to sound like me already). The pattern is the same every time; demand an answer from me (and not receive one), find an answer within yourself and then show contrition and desire to improve. Once you have passed through those three stages then I know you have become indoctrinated with the way I want you to think and then and only then will I end the silence. Well, perhaps, another week won't hurt me will it?

. I enjoy using silence because my first deployment of it indoctrinates you to a way of thinking. There are, however, other reasons why I enjoy it.

Firstly, I don't have to do anything. Yes that's right. I don't have to say or do a thing. I just walk away and stay away from you. I love anything that saves me energy whilst provoking a reaction in you and that is why the silent treatment is one of my favourite, if not my favourite method of getting to you. I also know that you won't just shrug your shoulders and think "Oh well, he will get in touch when he is ready to, I will just get on with my life."

I know this because your type just does not do that. You care about other people so if you think something is wrong (and especially if you then begin to think that you are the cause) you will do anything you can to try and ascertain what has happened and then repair it. That means that you will not stay away. You see, I have it all worked out.

Secondly, once I have given you a concentrated and potent dose of the silent treatment you will be ever anxious to avoid a repeat. It is not so much the fact of me being silent with you (in a way you might welcome it as it makes a change from my temper and the incessant criticisms that I send your way) that troubles you. No, it is the fact that you do not know why I am doing it that makes it so effective. As an empathic person, you are very good at showing understanding when somebody is upset or troubled. You can latch onto those feelings, relate them to your own experiences or because of your ability, you can imagine what it must be like to feel that way. Admirable indeed. In order for you to unleash the power of your empathy however you need to know what is wrong. It may only take a sentence but you still need to know. That thirst for knowledge is pretty incessant with you empaths and it pushes you to keep asking and trying to work out (see Obsessing) what is going on. Thus, if I manufacture a situation where you do not know the reason why I am treating you in this fashion, it will really hurt and confuse you.

The silent treatment really gets to you. You hate it so much you will always be alert to it happening again. This puts you in a state of hyper vigilance. You cannot settle. You are anxious. You are always looking to see if there is a trigger for it happening again. You start to try and second-guess me to ensure what you are about to say or what you are about to do won't result in you being consigned to silence again. Thus you become compliant and will do what I want in order to keep silence at bay. Very effective wouldn't you say?

I asked that management consultant what was the longest period of time he subjected someone to his silent treatment. He paused to recollect and then smiled the smile of someone very pleased with himself.

"About a minute."

I laughed out loud. Amateur.

16. Withdrawal

Although silence falls within a form of withdrawal, there are other ways in which I deploy withdrawal. I bring out withdrawal once I know that you have developed a degree of dependency on me. The supposed closeness that I once exhibited towards you will now be removed. I no longer have to shower you with affection nor do I have to take you to interesting places or buy you delightful things. Instead, I can pull away from you and that causes you to try and hold on tighter thus admiring me all the more and reacting with a greater degree. This reaction then feeds my need for fuel. I like to use withdrawal as it requires little effort on my part and you will now be acquainted with my desire to conserve energy. Taking you away for the weekend required the consumption of my resources of time and money. Not taking you (especially after I have promised to do so - Promised Gains) does not consume any of my resources at all. I just do nothing.

Deploying this tactic is easy. Whereas once I used to compliment you daily, I stop doing so. Once upon a time I would bring you a cup of tea in bed, now that does not happen. In fact, you find yourself bringing me a cup of tea in the hope that it might remind me or encourage me to do the same for you (who is Projecting now I wonder?). As it is well known, even if the description is a pathetic fallacy, nature abhors a vacuum and so do you. When I create this empty space by withdrawing my interest and affection from you, you try to bring it back to fill the empty space. This results in you trying ever harder to please me and as a consequence you give me more attention and admiration. You may also mourn this loss by pleading with me, crying or becoming angry. It is all a reaction so that gets approval from me.

The most effective method of withdrawal however is in the bedroom. In common with many narcissists (although admittedly not all) I am a sexual champion. I know you hate admitting this but you know that making love with me was the best that you ever had. In the Love Bombing phase I apply every pleasing technique I know. Someone of my nature has had a lot of sexual partners. This equates to lots of practice but more importantly it means that I have had lots of subjects to study in terms of how they react to my erotic overtures. I do not fall into the trap of assuming that my current partner will like the same thing as the previous one. Owing to this experience, I am not a one trick pony. Instead, if I note that one particular technique is not having the desired effect, I will switch to a different one. If that does not work either I have plenty more I can use until I hit the jackpot. Remember, I am highly skilled at reading you and therefore I pay close attention to how you react to the ways I might use my mouth, tongue, fingers et al. All of this makes me an accomplished and memorable lover.

In your mind of course this smorgasbord of sexual excellence tells you two things. I am totally into you and you have met your complete sexual match. It feels so damn good. We have to be soul mates for someone to bring out these reactions in you and as with much of my affection, it is utterly addictive. My female kin make particular use of this skill as a highly sexed agent of lust. Yes, I have read the comments from men about how much they miss the sexual energy of the female narcissist. I suppose that many men still expect that they should take the lead in matters sexual. The female narcissist turns that on its head and thus the allure and excitement increases.

Whether your narcissist is male, female or transgender you will be hooked on what goes on between the sheets. For many of us however, being a sexual Olympian was purely part of the Love Bombing. We actually find it a maintenance chore as repeated congress with someone becomes too much for us to bear. That degree of closeness over too long a period makes us feel very uncomfortable. Accordingly, we cannot actually wait to stop it and when we do we know that this form of withdrawal will hit you hard. It will strike you very hard indeed.

You equate sex with love. If I no longer touch you or make love to you, you feel unloved and this withdrawal pains you considerably. You want to recover it and also as I have explained you need to know what has caused this cessation of desire so you can unleash your empathy powers. This is another double whammy. You try to resurrect the passion by buying enticing lingerie, watching more porn or suggesting we watch it together (I prefer to do that alone to be honest). You rustle up plenty of ways that you find in the various self-help manuals about how to spice up your sex life. Those books are for relighting the fire of a healthy relationship that has gone or out or diminished as a consequence of familiarity with one another or the demands of a modern lifestyle getting in the way. Those publications will not help you with someone who has made a conscious decision to take away the most dazzling and enticing strand to our relationship.

The effect is the same. You ramp up the attention or your frustration manifests in arguments and entreatments to "just talk to me about it". It is all attention and just what I want.

If I am feeling sadistic I will grant you your wish and take you to bed. I may go through the motions and be robotic so that your initial euphoria at having persuaded me (what's this? A victory for you for once? Not so fast!) to conjoin with you soon fades, as I exhibit none of the skill and dedication I once did. Alternatively, I will flick that switch and engage the sexual athlete again. Wow, you had nearly forgotten how utterly delicious this is. Having been deprived of it for so long its effect is multiplied. You have got it back, you did it. As with everything I do, I am merely flying as high as I can to ensure the forthcoming drop is as far and hard as possible. As you lie back panting from our exertions, body all aglow in post-orgasmic delight you feel great. You want to curl up together, just as we used to and feel my fingers through your hair as we talk. I can barely contain my sense of euphoria at the impending power surge. I do not turn to you and hold you but instead I turn my back on you and face the other way or get up and go and sleep in the spare room. The effect is devastating. You thought I had given you what you wanted only for it to be snatched away at the last moment. I reinforce who has the power and upper hand in this relationship as your tears fall onto the pillow.

17. Boundary Violation

I am worse than an invading army when it comes to crossing lines and ignore conventions. What is behind my failure to respect other people's privacy and boundaries? It is because of my huge sense of entitlement and that I regard everyone else as an object or an appliance that is there to serve my purpose. I am unable and unwilling to distinguish between what belongs to you and what belongs to me. This is because I do not see any distinction between you and me. You are but an extension and you are there to do my bidding. I have to be involved in anything and everything that you do. Owing to my god-like status I am entitled to pass judgement on what you say, do, think and feel. My aim is to possess you. I will not acknowledge your independent existence from me, but instead I regard you as mine. By failing to acknowledge any boundaries between us then I can subsume you within me. This penetrative violation tells you who is in control and ensures that you will do what I want.

As with many of my manipulative techniques by doing this over and over, you eventually become conditioned to it. You lose your sense of self. You accept that what is yours is also mine. You cease to do things, which might set you apart from me, and instead you embrace that this is just the way it is. If I have been particularly charming, you will con yourself that all of this violation is because I love you so much. It is because I want us to meld together and become one. You have found a rare truth from me there. I do want us to become one. I want you to disappear into me and never be seen again. I want you to do what I want and when I want. I want you to look at the world with my skewed and malignant vision so that you automatically act and respond in the most appropriate way to feed my needs.

I see no boundaries anywhere I go. I talk to people how I like. I do not show respect to someone in authority. I see it as perfectly acceptable to embrace the wife of a friend full on the lips the first time we meet (she seems like a perfect candidate for some Love Bombing and Triangulation incidentally). I blaze through life knocking down fences; cutting through wires and ripping up the 'do not walk on the grass' signs. My sense of entitlement is so huge it knows no stopping.

How does this boundary violation manifest? I will tell you what you should wear. I will order for you when we go out for a meal. If someone asks you what you think about a certain political development, I will answer for you and you will smile and nod in agreement, thanking me for putting it so eloquently. I will go through your phone, open your post and read you diary. If you ever try and challenge me I will of course accuse you of trying to hide things from me and unleash a good old blast of Projection to make you feel bad and back down.

You will shop at certain stores and buy certain brands. I do not care that you have always used a certain shampoo; you must buy this one instead now. Of course, I will dress it up as me showing an interest.

"I love your hair, but I think it would look even better if you used this conditioner."

You are delighted that I have paid attention and I frame the violation in such a way that is appears to be a compliment, so you go along with it.

"I know you enjoy your steak well done, but have you considered trying it bloody? Someone with your heightened taste buds will really appreciate the difference."

So effective am I at doing this you will find yourself telling others about my recommendations and you will then even start to suggest them to your friends and family based on what I have said. Even when your best friend tells you,

"You've always hated green, it makes you look pale."

You will ignore these comments and plough on with what I have said.

It is an insidious method of control. I apply my boundary violations in a salami style, one slice at a time. What began as a pleasant suggestion as to how you should wear your hair then becomes me telling you which chair to sit in at dinner and whom you should socialise with. You will look back and wonder just how I managed to come to control every facet of your life by possessing you. It is simple. Each step I take is not sufficient in itself to alarm you and you accede to it. I push a bit further and again even if you have a feeling of discomfort, you think it will be silly to make a fuss about it. Little by little I take you over, crossing your lines, storming across your territory and occupying your life.

After a time I have possessed you. You do everything I want. I have invaded you and conquered you.

18. Gaslighting

You will be familiar with the origins of this technique. It arose from a stage play called "Gas Light". In this play, a manipulative husband wants to get rid of his wife and decides to do so by making her think she is losing her mind. He does this by effecting subtle alterations in her environment. One of these methods is dimming the flame on a gas lamp.

The term is now used to explain the technique that is used as a form of abusive manipulation. My aim is to generate such a high level of doubt in your mind that you will no longer trust your judgement about your life. The effect of this is that I diminish your self-esteem, I reduce your ability to assess in a rational and critical fashion what I am actually doing to you and I cause you to agree with what I assert thus enabling me to render you under my control. Once I have that control of course, you will behave precisely how I want so I can get my fuel from you.

To be effective in my gas lighting, I use a two-pronged approach. I must maintain an absolute conviction that what I am saying is the truth. I cannot waver from this. I must keep up this front at all times. I also need you to question your own position so that ultimately my united front succeeds.

I will apply such an unwavering intensity to what I say that you will find yourself thinking,

"He seems so convinced of what he is saying. To think like that he must be right yes?"

Bear in mind you are unlikely to know what I am or what I am doing. You will be perplexed by me maintaining a position which appears wrong, but you know I am an intelligent person and surely someone that clever would realise what they are saying is wrong? They must be right then if they keep saying it.

I will deploy indignation if you try and challenge me. I will make reference to previous points which I will distort to support my position. I will fire these observations and points at you in a rapid-fire irrefutable fashion. You will be caught in this hail of supposed facts that you will not be able to think clearly. You will be left spinning from the historical facts and struggle to recall whether they can be relied on or not. The more I gaslight you, the further your resolve weakens and you will even begin to believe that the distortions I have told you about are in effect true. The rigorous method by which this is applied will also cause you to feel drained and exhausted so that you will eventually not offer up any resistance.

This is an extreme form of psychological warfare. You will lose all trust in your own judgement and reality. When I first unleash this on you, you will notice that something odd is happening but you cannot quite put your finger on what it is. The subtlety of this manipulation is very effective. Keep in mind the fact that I have Love Bombed you so you will trust what I say. You will not want to think ill of anything I do. You will also be trying to recover the golden period which will result in your preferring not to rock the boat in anyway. All of this is excellent, fertile soil into which I can plant my gas lighting seeds. Everything I do in terms of manipulation is linked so that I can achieve the maximum effect and devastation.

What are some of the techniques that I use when gas lighting? I will say one thing and then deny it at a later stage. I will use my lieutenants to support me in this behaviour as well so that when you seek validation from a third party, you will find it absent. This is very effective. You may take the view I am wrong in what I have said and you may even have the presence of mind still to think I am doing this on purpose to prove a point. If a third party (who apparently is impartial) backs up my version of events then the doubt starts to creep in.

I will identify where you keep certain objects and if you keep them in the same place, such as your mobile phone charger of house keys. I will move them and when you cannot find them and set off searching, I will move them back to the usual place and then point this out to you. You will claim you had already checked the usual place and I will tell you that you could not have done since if you had you would have seen them.

I will also use a direct style once the gas lighting is beginning to have an effect whereby I will tell you that you are mistaken, or you are imagining things or that you look tired and it must be affecting your memory.

Over time your recall and perception is affected to such a degree that you will eventually accept what I say to be the truth of the matter. Once I realise I have achieved this I can roll out the huge lies in order to get away with whatever behaviour I want. I often wish I was an identical twin. That would be fantastic. I could appear in one place and say something and then be somewhere else a few minutes later which would easily take an hour to get to. How have I done that? I will deny the first conversation has ever taken place and suggest to you that you are seeing things. How could I have been at that train station a few minutes ago when I am in a bar across the city centre? That would really have a massive effect.

Ultimately, my gas lighting of you will render you unable to fight back and compliant with what I want, which in turn will feed my sense of power and give me the fuel that I need.

19. Circular Conversations

I use this in the context of an argument. They are endless and I repeat the same points over and over again with there being no resolution. What I manage to do is sucker you into thinking that you might be able to change my position and so you keep going. Remember, as someone who is strong on empathy you have an overwhelming desire to try and 'fix' me, even though that is impossible. You really believe that eventually I will 'see the light' and understand the error of my ways. What you need to understand is that I know what I am doing, I understand what I am doing but I do not care that what I do hurts other people and especially you. The ends always justify the means with me.

I have also created a false reality and therefore if you attempt to demonstrate something, which will interfere with this false reality I just will not accept it. I will claim that black is white and then the following day that it is orange. You cannot comprehend how I can maintain that position. It defies all logic. You know however that I am an intelligent person so how can it be that I cannot see this? You wonder whether perhaps you have not presented the situation in the clearest way. Maybe if you shout I might understand the point you are making? You are grounded in logic so you will keep going and going in order to try and make me see.

These conversations will go round and round and round. My behaviour will never change. More often than not the behaviour that you are challenging is not behaviour that should actually need to be raised with a healthy adult.

> "Why do you come in after 3am every Friday night?"
>
> "Why wasn't this bill paid?"
>
> "Why are you chatting with other women online?"

How do these circular conversations go? You will point something out and at first a reasoned discussion commences. This will go on for a short while and then you think that the issue has been resolved only for me to say something that shows it has not. My response will generally lack logic and be inflammatory. You then cannot accept this and you need to ensure I understand the point you are making so you repeat yourself. I make it feel as if the first conversation never happened as you make the same point and I counter them by not paying any attention to the legitimacy of what you are saying. This confuses and irritates you.

> "Did you not just hear what I said?"
>
> "Did any of what I said actually go into your head?"
>
> "I've already told you about this."

I will recite the usual excuses, which often do not make any sense to you and round and round it goes until you give up or lose your temper.

Not only are these conversations circular in nature they will also keep cropping up. This becomes doubly infuriating for you. The conversation itself goes round and round. There may not be any resolution within the conversation but you at least think the point has been made and I won't do the same thing again. However, I will. The same behaviour is committed again and therefore it is as if the circular conversation never happened. You point out the error of my ways and off we go again. It is akin to the moon spinning on its own axis whilst going around the earth in the same orbit. There are two doses of circularity.

I am doing this because I know that you will give up before I do. You will become exhausted and stop making the point. This exhaustion then lessens your defences so I can follow up the use of Circular Conversations with an alternative method of manipulation. It also reinforces my superiority. I am right and that makes me feel powerful. If you were criticising something I had done, you have failed to persuade me that I was wrong and therefore I am validated to do it again. I am also trying to provoke you. Eventually your frustration with getting nowhere will spill over. You will start to shout or you will slam a door. You may storm off. This is all good fuel for me. It also confirms that my technique is effective so I will keep using it as I know it gets to you. I will also make a mental note (or I may even add it to my notebook) of your unacceptable behaviour so I can bring it up on another occasion.

"I'm not having this discussion with you again because last time you stormed off in a huff. There is no point in me trying to reason with you because you will only do the same again and I find that hurtful."

I am also doing this to deflect responsibility and also accountability as by now you know full well that these are two things I do not accept. I regard the circular conversation as a competition. One whereby my ultimate aim is to never accept the logic of what you are saying, where I never accept I am to blame and I want you tired and frustrated by the incessant going round and round.

I demonstrate an amazing ability to keep talking and talking to maintain the circular conversation something, which will irritate the hell out of you when you have been subjected to some Silent Treatment as well. How can someone so talkative suddenly become utterly incommunicative? It is all about the manipulation you see. The games are always, I repeat, always being played. The sooner you realise that I am the master at the manipulative games the more chance you have of protecting yourself and avoiding the damage that comes with them.

In the case of circular conversations I suggest you find a brick wall and slam your head against it repeatedly. It will certainly prove more rewarding than going on the merry go round with me.

20. Everpresence

This is a pleasing consequence of all the hard work I invested in the Love Bombing technique. In order to overload your senses and sweep you up in my enticing whirlwind of love and affection I did numerous things to ensnare you.

I took you to a park and kissed you beneath a spreading oak tree, pushing you gently against the trunk as I whispered in your ear that this was our tree and we would always come back here and kiss beneath its huge boughs. I ensured that several songs became indelibly imprinted in your mind to remind you of you and me being together. I just didn't go for the romantic ones though. No, I ensured that I selected a range of music to accompany every mood and emotion. That upbeat dance track that is associated with our marvellous holiday in Ibiza. That slow waltzing song that we held each other to and listened to on the balcony of my apartment. That frenetic and energetic rock track that we both jumped around to in your living room. You marvelled at how I managed to select certain songs and pieces of music that you loved and seemed so apt for the moment we were caught up in. You did not know that I had already spent time studying the YouTube videos of songs you adore on your Facebook news feed. I have also wheeled out this playlist to several other victims and I know it works.

I made sure that you would repeatedly see me sat in the same seat in your kitchen reading a Terry Pratchett book. You would then make dinner as I read aloud to you. We always had a bottle of Rioja on a Wednesday evening. I selected four particular restaurants and took you to them repeatedly. I engaged my lieutenants in reinforcing all the wonderful memories associated with dinner parties, trips to the coast and sporting events. Every day there would be a poem left for you under your pillow. I devoured box sets of Breaking Bad, Poldark and West Wing with you. I even learned pieces of the dialogue, which I would repeat from time to time.

I specifically wore the same fragrance, used the same anti-perspirant and shower gel so that this created a particular cocktail of scents, which are forever linked to me. My washing powder and fabric conditioner were chosen to stand out for you. Little do you know I have a notebook, which lists each ex-girlfriend and a corresponding list of smells that I used when I was with you. For you it was Chanel Allure Sport, Dove Men and Care Clean deodorant and Molton Brown Black Peppercorn Body Wash. Not that you have forgotten that have you?

The dedication by which I ensured I had imprinted myself on your life in every conceivable sense was worthwhile. Not only did I draw you in and ensnare you, but I also left my mark on you so that once I had discarded you (or if you made the bold move of leaving me) I would forever remain with you.

You walk through the park and you are haunted by the image of us up against the oak tree. Somebody gets in the lift next to you wearing Chanel Allure and you want to reach out and hug him as you are immediately taken back to smelling me lying next to you in bed. When *With or Without You* is played you start to sob as you recall how I held you close during a thunderstorm as it played in the background (on repeat of course). Everything I did during the Love Bombing was calculated to trap you but was also laying the ground for infecting the afterwards with me. You see me in books, taste me in certain foods and hear my voice when watching a re-run of a programme. You try to escape by avoiding certain things that are poignant reminders, but that means cutting out certain things that you enjoy. Should you make that sacrifice to someone like me? You are torn. Even if you exercise such discipline, I have planted enough reminders around you that you cannot and will not escape me.

You go to the newsagents and see The Times newspaper and instantly remember show I would read it on a Sunday as we lounged after making love through the morning. The powerful memory hurts. I am a spectre that follows you everywhere you go. I know this is happening and it gives me a wonderful sense of omnipotent power. I know that I am in your head and heart on a daily basis. I know how much pain this will be causing you. I also know that I still have several hooks deep inside you and it will not take much if I decided to throw a line to you to draw you back in.

- Such an attention to detail has reaped several rewards.
- I drew you in.
- I remain with you through my ever presence.
- I cause you pain.
- I feel omnipotent.
- I have the means to draw you in again, like a sleeper cell planted inside you.

It is stunningly effective and in the phase of ever presence I do not actually have to do anything because the hard work was done many months ago during my Love bombing of you.

If your life happened to be a crime scene my DNA would be found all over it.

21. Pity

The world operates on pity. It is a cousin of love. How many times have you watched a moving advertisement on television for an abused child or a starving child in an under-developed nation? As those strings play in the soundtrack, your heart strings are also being played to make a donation. You pity the poor wretch for the awful situation he or she finds his or herself in. You pity the poor, the refugees, the homeless, the sick, the dying, the abused and the uprooted. Your sense of pity rises each time so you are compelled to act. You know you cannot reach out and hug that person so you reach out and make a donation. The charities and appeals all know that you are capable of showing such compassion and pity and they embrace it.

I know that demonstrating the empathy that you do, you will be brimming with pity and compassion. It is figuratively spilling from you, just waiting to be poured on to some poor, deserving soul. You cannot help but want to show you care, that you understand and that you can step into the shoes of the victim and help them by demonstrating your pity for them.

I exploit this by drinking deep on your pity. I use the masks of misfortune and victimisation so that I can guilt-trip you into feeling sorry for me. I make you believe that I am suffering more than you are. I position myself as a poor and helpless victim yet I am far from that. By taking this step, I am actually wielding a power over you. I am right to do this because I am entitled to this pity.

I never consider the consequences of what I do. I have no regard for accountability or responsibility. It is my mission to make you feel responsible for my situation. You will be made to feel guilty if you do not pity me and help me or take my side.

I will trot out some calamitous tale to you. Often it is imaginary but I know you are a sucker for a sob story. Not only will I lay it on thick I will always make it seem worse for me. I will even do it when I know you are suffering yourself. You are barely able to move owing to a savage dose of flu. I sneeze once and expect you to come running for me. You could have a severed artery and I will expect you to apply a band aid to the tiny scratch on my arm.

I will play the victim. I will turn situations around so that I make myself the victim and if you try and deny that status to me, I will denigrate you for your selfishness and lack of compassion for me. Given that compassion and pity are central tenets of your being, you will struggle not to fall for my overtures. I play on what makes you tick and being Florence Nightingale appeals massively to your nature.

Once again by obtaining your pity, I have you doing what I want, giving me attention and often to the detriment of yourself. Indeed, I specialise in ensuring that you ultimately put my needs before your own. That begins a downward spiral for your health and well being.

22. Isolation

I cannot stand being on my own. I must avoid it. Instead I want you to be isolated (straight into some Projection there). I require your isolation for two reasons:-

1.   So I have you all to myself so that all your attention is focussed on me and nobody or anything else; and

2.   This vastly reduces the risk of third party interference, which might bring you to your senses

The isolation commences during the Love Bombing phase. I want to spend as much time as possible with you for the reasons I have outlined in the first manipulative technique above. This ensures that I have plenty of fuel from you. I will achieve this isolation in several ways.

I spend all my time with you so you do not have the time to do anything else. I will alienate you from your friends by identifying the weaknesses they have and exploiting them.

"Amanda talks about you behind your back you know; I don't know why you are friends with her."
"You know, I think John is a secret alcoholic. You can do better than socialising with him."
"Lucy is a deadbeat. Her career is going nowhere and she is unreliable. You don't want someone like that in your life. You deserve much better than her."

"Rachel keeps trying to hit on me (of course it is the other way around). You need to watch out for her. Maybe it would be better if you didn't invite her around so often."

I dress all of this up as concern for you as I look to drive a wedge between you and your friends.

I won't want you working either. I will play the guilt card and suggest to you that the children need you at home and therefore you should not work. Alternatively, I will tell you that I earn enough for the two of us and you deserve to enjoy leisure time (after you have worked so hard previously) and you run the home so well. A touch of flattery works well of course.

If you consider helping out at some charity or volunteer group I will say,

"That's really admirable but I think the children need their mum more than the charity needs you don't they? There are plenty of other people who can help the charity but nobody can be a mum to our children like you can they?"

A coercive dollop of guilt bundled up with some flattery.

If I take the view that you need to work to bring in the money I will criticise your colleagues and suggest that they take advantage of you. This is done to prevent you from going to any social activity that involves work. I will also come out with comments such as:-

"You work hard; you should stay at home more."
"The children miss you. I know you have to work and we all appreciate that but it would be better if they saw more of their mum rather than you going out with people who see you every day as it is."

"I miss you. Can't we do something together instead?" (Which invariably means sitting watching television whilst I get you to run around after me? If you complain I will guilt trip you by saying I hardly see you and you do more for the people you work with than for me, the person you apparently love.)

    I may sell your car so that you are less able to go anywhere and meet people and do it under the apparently laudable banner of economising or even looking out for the environment. I will forbid you from using public transport instead as it is not safe. I may remove the modem from the house when I am not there so you are not able to access the internet, feigning that it was broken or I needed it elsewhere. I will ensure that all communications that come your way are vetted and seen by me (Boundary Violation) to enable me to then disparage that communication in the expectation you will not reply or become fearful of receiving further communications so you advise the sender not to get in touch with you.

    I may suggest moving away from the area. This works a treat from wrenching you away from all of your friends, family and colleagues. When we start in the new place I will lay down firm rules from the beginning, which will have the effect of isolating you straight away and I will keep you in that state of isolation. If you try to change it, I will accuse you of ruining our new start.

    By isolating you I prevent any voice of reason from ruining my plans to have complete control of you. I am far more able to brainwash you into doing what I want (giving me lots of fuel) if my voice is the only voice that you hear. I also ensure that you become completely dependent on me. Those who once socialised will give up trying because you never reply to messages or I tell them that you cannot attend.

I will also ensure that if you plan on going somewhere I cause such a fuss that it always becomes a battle. I will trot out plenty of lines to make you feel guilty, criticise those you are going out with, demean the way you dress and how much make-up you have on so that it becomes so tiring trying to deal with this incessant awkwardness and nastiness on my part that you decide it is not worth the aggravation and don't go.

By cutting you off from everyone else, nobody can point out to you what I am doing. I become your world and since I build a false reality for you to exist in, nobody is going to come along and disturb that. I have you trapped in this fictional construct where you are even more susceptible to all of my other manipulative techniques. You are also so dependent on me for the simple reason that because of this isolation you are completely terrified of losing me.

23. Bringing Up the Past

Let me say straight away that this is my book about manipulative techniques. It is not yours. So you are never allowed to bring up the past in order to chastise, criticise or prove a point to me. Oh no. Naturally, I am perfectly entitled to do this in order to manipulate you. Hypocrisy and me just get along fine, don't you know.

For someone that cannot repeatedly recall what has happened maybe just two days ago (see Gas lighting) I suddenly develop amazing powers of recall (here's my contradictory nature again) in order to rake up the past. If I am a parent to you, I will do it in order to make you feel like a small, defenceless child again (although I am actually Projecting as well as to how I feel). I will bring up the fact you failed a particular exam twenty years ago or make mention of how you used to wet the bed until you were aged 9. I do not bring up these past matters as an affectionate bit of poking fun at you, I do it to remind you that I am the one in control.

I pick something visceral and often unresolved for you so that you are swept straight back to your childhood and the shame envelopes you. You hate me for doing it but I am reminding you of something that actually happened. There is no relevance in mentioning it now, but that does not matter to me. Using this technique is another method of manipulating you into feel inferior to me and enabling me to exert control over you.

I also use it as a method of deflection to avoid having to be accountable for my behaviour. I stagger in drunk for the umpteenth weekend in a row. This means I will be hung over again tomorrow and I won't want to do anything with you. You point out how selfish and inconsiderate my behaviour is. I will not accept this even though it is obvious. Instead, I will make reference to the fact that eight months ago you once returned absolutely hammered at 2am. I will leave out the fact that this was your first night out in six months (as I had been giving Isolation a real good go) or the fact that you were celebrating your sister's twenty-first birthday. That is forgotten. I will focus on the fact that you vomited and made a mess in the bathroom. I on the other hand have never made a mess in the bathroom and thus I bring up this solitary and distant transgression to deflect from my own behaviour and make you feel bad.

"You are drunk again, this happens every weekend. You go out with your friends and have a skin full and then stagger in here. You ruin the next day and we were meant to be going to the lake for the day."

"Oh give it a rest. I am just enjoying myself. You never let me enjoy myself. Maybe if you were nicer to me I would not have to keep going out. Have you thought about that?"

"What are you talking about? I am always pleasant to you?"

"Really? Well what about that time you came in drunk and you spewed all over the bathroom. What a mess and the smell was, good lord, what had you been eating? It was disgusting."

"That was the once and I had not been out in ages."

"It was one time too many. It was horrible. You made a right show of yourself."

"No I didn't."

"How can you remember? You were drunk. The one time you go out and look what a state you get in. Is it any wonder that I am reluctant to agree to you going out? I do it for your own good."

"That was ages ago. I have not done it since."

"That doesn't matter. It was bad enough then and it is a good job you have not repeated it. You were a disgrace."

By dragging up the past about your behaviour, I have shifted the emphasis onto you. I have forced you to defend your actions and made you out to be the bad one. All talk of my late and drunken arrival is forgotten as you are forced to defend yourself against my unwarranted attack from your isolated incident of drunkenness.

Another useful effect that arises from me using this technique is that you become conditioned to trying to ensure I have no further ammunition to bring up later on. Accordingly, you start to regulate your behaviour in such a way that you try and second guess what I might remember and criticise you for. This allows me to exert further control over you. You are fearful that something you might do will be remembered by me and used against you at a later stage.

I also know that you crave safety and security. In bringing up the past I am reminding you that the status quo can easily be damaged by your behaviour and that I have not forgotten or forgiven you for what you have done. You need to double your efforts to please me otherwise there may be repercussions (I am adding a dusting of Threatened Loss here as well).

I like to make use of two particular words as well when bringing up the past. You would do well to look out for those words as they are key indicators that I am deploying this manipulative technique. They are the words "always" and "never".

"You always forget to bring me a cup of tea in the morning."

Thus I am reinforcing that this has happened in the past before.

"You never hug me last thing at night these days."

Accordingly, I am reminding you of a good thing that you used to do in the past but you are no longer doing. Keep an eye out for the use of these words as they show clearly what I am doing.

24. Rage

This is a blunt instrument but it is also a method of manipulation. If you criticise me in any way or you fail to give me the fuel that I crave, for instance you start talking about your injury and thus moving the spotlight onto you or you are spending time at a dinner party talking to other people, I will feel a huge injurious sense and this will invariably result in me unleashing my rage.

This can take several forms. It may be a set of barbed remarks sent in your direction, it could be a full blown shouted dressing down or even the use of physical violence. I dislike using physical violence beyond grabbing and holding as it tends to leave evidence and diminishes the successful prospects of maintain plausible deniability to con others you may turn to. Admittedly, there are those of my kind, usually those who are at the low-functioning end of the spectrum who are unable to keep their fists to themselves and they will lash out and administer a beating.

Whether this rage comes from shouting at you so you back into a corner curled up and afraid or whether it is a savage physical assault the purpose of it is to instil fear into you. Not only will you hate to be on the receiving end of my rage you also do not want other people to witness it for fear of them being upset by it. For instance, you do not want children to have to witness this behaviour, other family members, neighbours or colleagues. I do not care for any of that. This is because I am in my mind justified that I can and should lash out at you. You have caused this. Your behaviour was so inconsiderate to me that I am allowed to go on the attack in such a manner. I also have no regard for what others may think because of my innate superiority and my belief in my ability to charm them at a later stage if need be. This all means that there are no normal societal checks on my rage and it is able to have full vent. I cannot regulate my rage myself, I fear no admonishment by my peers or society and therefore like the flames from a dragon, you are subjected to its full heat and intensity.

This experience in itself is extremely unpleasant but it is the ever present fear of it happening again. Once you have tasted my rage you will not want to experience it again. Accordingly, this causes you to submit to my way of thinking. You will second guess how I might react to what you do to ensure that you do not unleash the beast within. You want to keep it tethered and under control. The nastiness that flows from my temper has to be avoided for your sake and those you care about around you. Thus, as usual, you instigate the compromise and back down. I get my way. Again.

25. Hope

I have left this to last and with good reason. After everything else that has happened. After every manipulative technique that I have deployed against you, I always have one final controlling flourish available to me. That is hope.

I am afraid this last technique relies as much on you as it does on me. Your empathic ways mean that you try and see the good in everyone. You are the eternal optimist. You believe that love can conquer all and that someone can always be saved. This viewpoint means that you place great stock in there being hope that I will change, that I will see the error of my ways, that I will have a moment of revelationary redemption and cease to treat you so badly.

I cultivate this hope by hinting that I want to be a better person that I am sorry for what I have done and that things can get better. I will give you those glimmers that we can return to the golden period once again and rekindle that perfect love that we seemed to have. You will still not have realised that my love for you did not exist and that you fell in love with an illusion.

This hope will keep you clinging to me. It ensures you try harder to please me and thus give me more fuel. This hope means you dare not leave just in case things do get better. You do not want to give up because you once looked upon a perfect love and although in the morning it was gone, you knew what you had seen and experienced and you want it back.

Hope is a powerful emotion. People hope that the missing child will be found and therefore will not give up searching. They hope their team will score an equalising goal and thus they continue to cheer and urge their team on. The doctors have hope that treatment will work to save somebody's life and therefore they keep trying different methods to achieve the right outcome. Hope is powerful and largely used to effect good. Unfortunately for you, the use of hope in our dynamic means only that you will stay with me and be subjected to my toxicity for longer.

Why do I use this technique and why do you keep hanging on or coming back to me? It is simple. Out of all your feelings and emotions for me, the one that stays right until the end is hope.

Hope dies last.

Conclusion

There you have it. Twenty-five powerful manipulative techniques that I deploy. You are now better placed to identify them before they happen or if you are in the middle of my nightmare world then you now know what is being done to you. Do not keep this precious knowledge to yourself encourage others to digest it so that they may be better protected.

This is not an exhaustive list of my techniques. There are others and perhaps I will share them with you too. Perhaps I will keep them to myself, who can say? Now that you are aware of these various techniques the next question presents itself. What can you do about them? Are you only ever able to avoid their effect by staying away from my kind and me? Must you see them coming and then take evasive action before they get a hold of you? The answers to how to deal with these various forms of manipulation can be found in my book **Escape: How to Beat the Narcissist.** You may wish to drink deep of the knowledge that can be found there. Thank you for reading.

Further publications by H G Tudor

Evil

Confessions of a Narcissist

More Confessions of a Narcissist

Further Confessions of a Narcissist

Narcissist:Seduction

Narcissist:Ensnared

From the Mouth of a Narcissist

Escape: How to beat the Narcissist

Danger : 50 Things You Should Not Do With a Narcissist

Departure Imminent: How to Prepare for No Contact and Beat the Narcissist

Chained : The Narcissist's Co-Dependent

Fuel

Knowing the Narcissist
Facebook page

@narcissist_me
Twitter

narcsite.wordpress.com
Blog

Printed in Great Britain
by Amazon